Student Internship Success Workbook:
20+ Lessons and Activities for
Student Intern
Career Readiness

By: Dr. Saby Labor

Resilient Campus LLC

This book is part of the *Student Internship Success Bundle*.
The supervisor's companion book is:
Student Internship Success Workbook:
20+ Lessons and Activities for
Student Intern Career Readiness
(Supervisor's Guide)

For more resources, visit:

www.studentinternshipsuccess.com

Welcome!

You have taken an important step toward your future as a professional and as a lifelong learner. Internship and employment opportunities provide rich environments for learning about yourself, the workplace, and other professionals and teams. This workbook provides you new content to grow your capacities as a student and professional in order to strengthen your practice of habits that will provide the foundation for your success in the years to come.

Who is this Workbook for?

The Student Intern Success Workbook is for college student interns and student employees. This workbook provides lessons and reflection activities centered on:

- Personal Foundations
- Professionalism
- Communication Skills
- Career Readiness

This workbook is a comprehensive resource for students enrolled in college success programs to support historically underrepresented students, such as TRiO, GEAR UP, Educational Opportunity Programs, among others.

Table of Contents

How This Workbook is Organized

Pre-Internship

This section includes activities and information about important topics to help you better prepare for your internship experience and your academic term.

Weekly Lessons

Each weekly lesson contains opportunities to deepen your knowledge in the following areas:

- Personal Foundations
- Professionalism
- Communication Skills
- Career Readiness

You can travel through this workbook each week or complete multiple lessons at your own pace.

Weekly Activities

There are suggested activities and reflection questions you can choose to participate in that will add value to the content learned in each weekly lesson.

Evaluation and Progress Tracking

A typical internship experience is 12-20 weeks in duration. Quarterly check-in points are provided throughout this workbook to promote self-reflection and solicit feedback from your supervisor. This provides opportunities to enhance your professional development throughout your internship. These shortened time periods will assist you in tracking your progress and accomplishments, monitoring goals and habits from quarter to quarter, and provide initial and final points for evaluation. Here is an example of quarterly check-in points that take place over a 16-week internship:

- Quarter 1: Week 1-4
- Quarter 2: Week 5-8 (Mid-Point)
- Quarter 3: Week 9-12
- Quarter 4: Week 13-16 (Final)
- Overall Reflection: Week 16

Post-Internship

This section includes resources, tips, and reflection activities to continue your growth and learning after you have completed your internship experience.

Making the Most of Your Internship Experience

Be Dependable

- Show up consistently
- Arrive early or on time
- Follow through
- Communicate clearly and consistently
- Be adaptable

Show Them What You're Made Of...

- Give each project 100% of your energy, focus, and abilities
- Be coachable
- Ask for clarification and additional information
- Be proactive in asking for new projects and assignments
- Offer to help with existing projects
- Carve out your space
- Demonstrate your interests and skills
- Establish your niche "expertise" area
- Offer ideas when asked
- Absorb all the information you can about the profession
- Demonstrate your teamwork skills
- Request possible meetings or professionals to shadow
- Conduct informational interviews with your supervisor and other professionals

Other Tips

Treat your internship like a job. Show up early, follow through on tasks that you are responsible for, and pretend as if you will give your paycheck back if you do not meet the expectations. This helps you develop a professional mindset of accountability to yourself and to others.

- Get organized
- Use all the tools you have access to
- Create to-do lists
- Track your time

Making the Most of Your Internship Experience
Practice Self-Reflection

Journaling, taking notes, writing questions, and reflecting on how you are interacting and growing are all important professional strategies to practice.

Setting a Schedule

Keep all your roles and responsibilities in mind when setting your schedule. You have 168 hours each week.

> *Class time + homework and study time + work + internship +*
> *travel time + sleeping + eating + personal time… (you get the point…)*

Time flies once the semester starts. Planning wisely can increase your stability during peak times. Here are some strategies to plan wisely during your internship experience.

Planning Ahead With Your Supervisor:
- Schedule your weekly check-in meeting
- Schedule your mid-point check-in meeting
- Schedule your final check-in meeting

Tools for a Healthy Scheduling Habit

Daily calendar: Keep a detailed daily schedule. You can download printable calendar templates online or use an online calendar app on your smart phone.

Developing Career Readiness Competencies

Employers are seeking professionals with these skills:
- Critical thinking and problem solving
- Professionalism
- Teamwork and collaboration
- Oral and written communication
- Information technology
- Leadership
- Career management

(Source: National Association of Colleges and Employers)

Pre-Internship: Before You Get Started...

What is an Internship?

An internship is an opportunity to gain experience within an organization and within the professional world. Internships can be paid or unpaid, for academic credit and non-credit bearing opportunities as well. The duration of internships varies; some take place only in the summer, during one semester, or even one year. An internship is often your chance to ask questions and learn more about what skills and knowledge are needed for professional positions in a particular field.

Purpose

There are several purposes of internships. For student interns, learning more about possible career paths, professionalism, and building a portfolio of experience are just a few of the key purposes of internships. For employers, internships provide an opportunity to train and mentor the incoming professionals of their organization or field, as well as obtaining additional project and task-specific help from student interns.

What to Expect

Pace: There are peak and off-peak times for workplace activity and productivity. Expect to have periods of time when the pace of projects, tasks, or office life is very quick, and also expect times when the pace is slower.

Rigor: An internship is your opportunity to demonstrate your skills, strengths, and knowledge to potential future colleagues and employers. This is your chance to learn as much as you can, ask questions, take notes, and learn new skills. Show them your best self and your best work!

Learning Curve: The early period of an internship involves a significant amount of information and learning new routines of office life, new names of colleagues, and adapting to a new schedule and commute. Take notes, ask questions, and do your best to adjust to the new routine.

Pre-Internship: Before You Get Started...

Habits

Habits are like a muscle.
You build and strengthen habits through repetition.
It is incredibly difficult to re-train and re-condition poorly formed habits, so developing health habits is an essential strategy for success.

How Long Does It Take To Form a Habit?

A study by Phillippa Lally, a health psychologist, found that a habit forms after 66 days on average of implementation. The study also highlighted that you don't have to be perfect. Some participants missed a day or two, and were able to continue practicing the habit before it was formed.

Strategies to Develop Habits

- Start with easy habits
- Increase habits in small increments
- Break it down into very easy pieces
- Focus on performing the habit, rather than focusing on the outcome
- If you miss a day, just pick back up where you left off

Weekly Habits

Establish healthy and effective habits to promote success.
Preparing for the week on Saturday or Sunday by looking ahead at your week's schedule, big events and due dates, and starting your week off with enough sleep are habits that promote success!

Reflection Activity

Name one habit that promotes success in your personal life...

Name one habit that promotes success in your academic life...

Name one habit that promotes success in your professional life...

Pre-Internship: Before You Get Started...

Goals and habits are connected. While goals are helpful for determining your direction and objective, your habits make up the system you will follow to make progress on these goals.

Goal Setting System

It is important to set specific goals that are measurable and realistic. Keep in mind the SMART goals method:

- **S**pecific
- **M**easurable
- **A**ttainable
- **R**ealistic
- **T**ime-bound

Implementation Intentions

Break large goals down into daily habits and when possible, connect them to tasks In your daily routine. Make a plan for when, where, and how you will accomplish your goals.

For example, "After I brush my teeth in the morning, I will journal for 7 minutes in my room about 3 things I am grateful for and 3 intentions for the day."

By determining intentions to implement your smaller habits and goals, you will be closer to achieving larger goals.

Tips for Success

- **Showing up for your goals and habits is essential**. Be sure to track how often you are showing up and what you perform during this time.
- **Align your environment with your goals and habits**. Determine the conditions that support you showing up for your goals and habits, then make decisions to alter your existing environment or seek environments that more closely match these conditions.
- **Use visual cues in your environment.** These serve to remind you, or to directly support the behavior you want.
- **Share your goals with others.** This creates an accountability system and system of support for yourself.

Pre-Internship: Setting Your Intentions
Goals

Set 3 goals to achieve this semester. Remember the SMART model for goal setting. Write your goals below:

Goals	Progress Notes
1. *Personal*	
2. *Academic*	
3. *Professional*	

Habits

Name 3 habit you will work to develop this semester. Write them below:

Habits	Progress Notes
1. *Personal*	
2. *Academic*	
3. *Professional*	

Pre-Internship: Setting Your Expectations
Reflection Activity:
What expectations do you have of your supervisor?

What is your preferred mode of communication for professional purposes?
- Email
- Phone
- In-person

What do you expect to get out of this experience?

How will you contribute to your own success?

Learning Your Supervisor's Expectations
Discuss these questions with your supervisor:

What expectations does your supervisor have of you?

What is your supervisor's preferred mode of communication?

How will you supervisor contribute to your success?

Pre-Internship: Communication Skills

Interpersonal Communication Skills

- Attentiveness
- Listening
- Asking questions
- Showing interest
- Facial and body language
- Verbal language

Written Communication

There are a variety of formats for written communication. Emails, newsletters, letters, and memos are just a few examples.

Communication Tips

Here are some tips you can use to practice professional written communication:

- State your purpose
- Know your audience
- Use proper tone, grammar, and punctuation for the intended audience
- Step away from a written document and return later to edit and adjust the format

Learning Styles

How you and others process information is an essential ingredient in professional communication. There are many different models for understanding learning styles.

Here is a simple model that describes three learning styles:

- Visual: Learn by seeing
- Auditory: Learn by hearing
- Physical or Kinesthetic: Learn by doing and physical movement

Want to know your learning style? Take the online quiz listed here to find out: http://www.howtolearn.com/learning-styles-quiz

Write your learning style preference here: _____

_____% Visual

_____% Auditory

_____% Physical or Kinesthetic

Week 1: Professionalism and Work Ethic

Answering Phones
- Have a pen and notepad nearby the phone to take messages
- Familiarize yourself with the message needed to answer the phones
- Practice transferring calls, using the hold function, and using multiple lines of a phone
- Talk slowly and clearly when answering and speaking on the phone
- Smile (it warms up your tone) and sit comfortably and upright

Computer Etiquette
- Your personal laptop or tablet should not be visible
- Only use social media (Facebook, Twitter, and others) during your break times (unless your internship responsibilities include managing the organization's social media accounts)
- Music or earphones are usually not appropriate in professional settings
- Use your professional account login while at your internship site
- Log off from this account when you step away from the computer
- Keep your organizational email account logged in and monitor it throughout the day

Personal Phone
- Keep your phone on silent and put away while working
- Make personal calls from your cell phone during break times and in areas where it won't disrupt the work of others

Other Professional Tips
- Arrive early and give yourself plenty of time to settle in before starting work promptly
- Always have a notepad and pen to take notes
- Keep your internship notes, projects, and lists in one common folder or notebook
- Ask about meetings, events, and other scheduling details and add to your calendar
- Wear your name badge regularly if provided one and always carry any keys or ID card with you for the workplace

Important note: *When in doubt about professional behavior and expectations, ask your supervisor for more information.*

Week 1: Onboarding Meeting   Date/Time_____

- Get to know each other
- Discuss expectations and preferred communication modes
- Determine weekly schedule for your internship
- Read through all materials provided and bring any remaining questions

Weekly Check-In Meeting   Date/Time_____

Check-In

Talk with your supervisor about how you are doing, how your classes are going, and how your internship is going so far.

Report Your Progress

Bring updates regarding your progress on completed tasks and projects, as well as progress on ongoing work. Take notes and repeat any timelines, due dates, and clarify expectations for task or project completion.

Ask for Feedback

Ask for feedback from your supervisor about what you are doing well and which areas you could improve your performance. Ask your supervisor for any resources or additional information to support any areas of growth .

Ask for Support

Ask your supervisor for additional resources or support to support your internship experience.

Celebrate

Celebrate your accomplishments and growth, even if they seem incremental at times.

Summarize

Take notes of any tasks, due dates, upcoming meetings and events, and any other important items in need of follow-up.

Week 2: Time Management

Tracking your time spent on various life activities, then ensuring you have systems in place that promote the best use of your time and energy will promote balance and productivity.

Time Management Tips

- Allot time based on your natural rhythm when possible (high energy activities at your body's natural high energy times)
- Re-purpose your down time between classes for studying or project work
- Set a schedule and stick to it (revisit and adjust your schedule periodically)
- Track small and large projects with to-do lists
- Monitor how much time is spent on social media, television, and online

Time Management Activity

Track each 15-minute block of time each day for one week to assess where your time is spent. Evaluate your time spent on each major area of your life and re-allocate any time between areas when needed.

Weekly Check-In Meeting   Date/Time_____

Check-In

Talk with your supervisor about how you are doing, how your classes are going, and how your internship is going so far.

Report Your Progress

Bring updates regarding your progress on completed tasks and projects, as well as progress on ongoing work. Take notes and repeat any timelines, due dates, and clarify expectations for task or project completion.

Ask for Feedback

Ask for feedback from your supervisor about what you are doing well and which areas you could improve your performance. Ask your supervisor for any resources or additional information to support any areas of growth .

Ask for Support

Ask your supervisor for additional resources or support to support your internship experience.

Celebrate

Celebrate your accomplishments and growth, even if they seem incremental at times.

Summarize

Take notes of any tasks, due dates, upcoming meetings and events, and any other important items in need of follow-up.

Week 3: Communication Styles
Introverts and Extroverts (Your energy source)
People are not simply either an introvert or an extrovert. They might have strong tendencies in one or the other, or even share strong tendencies in both.

- **Introverts** get their energy, or recharge their brain, from spending time alone. They lose energy by being around people for long periods of time.
- **Extroverts** get their energy from other people. They lose energy when spending too much time alone.

D.O.P.E. Personality Model
This model is a result of several research studies examining individual characteristics regarding these elements of personalities:

- Communication
- Assertiveness

- Emotionality
- Judging

In short, there are four personality styles (based on characteristics of birds for simplicity):

- DOVE "the harmony seeker"
- OWL "the detail seeker"

- PEACOCK "the excitement seeker"
- EAGLE "the results seeker"

Given a person's personality style, there are specific communication and interpersonal strategies recommended to maximize communication effectiveness.

Take the D.O.P.E. Bird Assessment located online. You can find the test for purchase at RichardStep.com. Select one answer for each question, then add up your total number of responses for each letter response.

Write your Communication Style here: _____

Reflection Activity
What are some ways that you can apply your learning and communication style in your daily life? In accomplishing your life goals?

Weekly Check-In Meeting   Date/Time_____

Check-In

Talk with your supervisor about how you are doing, how your classes are going, and how your internship is going so far.

Report Your Progress

Bring updates regarding your progress on completed tasks and projects, as well as progress on ongoing work. Take notes and repeat any timelines, due dates, and clarify expectations for task or project completion.

Ask for Feedback

Ask for feedback from your supervisor about what you are doing well and which areas you could improve your performance. Ask your supervisor for any resources or additional information to support any areas of growth .

Ask for Support

Ask your supervisor for additional resources or support to support your internship experience.

Celebrate

Celebrate your accomplishments and growth, even if they seem incremental at times.

Summarize

Take notes of any tasks, due dates, upcoming meetings and events, and any other important items in need of follow-up.

Week 4: Working with People of Different View Points

Definition of Empathy

The ability to see from another person's perspective with respect and understanding. You will encounter people with perspectives that are similar to and different from your own.

Dialogue vs. Debate

The goal of dialogue is to hear the perspective of others and develop understanding through mutual respect. The goal is not to change someone's opinion or to "win" (as is the goal in a debate).

The "Personal is Political"

It is challenging to hear viewpoints that negatively effect you or your communities without taking it personally. It is essential that you engage with others in a way that reinforces your own integrity and professionalism, and maintains openness and respect to other perspectives.

Strategies

Active Listening:

- Listen intently to the other person
- Align your verbal and non-verbal language with your message
- Ask questions with the goal of developing understanding
- Provide positive feedback
- Give others adequate time to respond
- Respect the rights of others to be heard
- Respect the efforts of others when they share
- Respect the viewpoint of others

Activity

Practice these empathy statements:
- "Thank you for sharing your viewpoint."
- "I can understand where you're coming from."
- "You have given me much to reflect on."

Weekly Check-In Meeting

Date/Time_____

Check-In

Talk with your supervisor about how you are doing, how your classes are going, and how your internship is going so far.

Report Your Progress

Bring updates regarding your progress on completed tasks and projects, as well as progress on ongoing work. Take notes and repeat any timelines, due dates, and clarify expectations for task or project completion.

Ask for Feedback

Ask for feedback from your supervisor about what you are doing well and which areas you could improve your performance. Ask your supervisor for any resources or additional information to support any areas of growth .

Ask for Support

Ask your supervisor for additional resources or support to support your internship experience.

Celebrate

Celebrate your accomplishments and growth, even if they seem incremental at times.

Summarize

Take notes of any tasks, due dates, upcoming meetings and events, and any other important items in need of follow-up.

Quarter 1 Check-In: Week 1-4
Goals
Re-state and evaluate your goals from the Pre-Internship section (page 9). Make any necessary adjustments and write them below.

Goals	Progress Notes
1. *Personal*	
2. *Academic*	
3. *Professional*	

Habits
Re-state and evaluate your habits from the Pre-Internship section (page 9). Make any necessary adjustments and write them below:

Habits	Progress Notes
1. *Personal*	
2. *Academic*	
3. *Professional*	

Quarter 1 Self-Reflection: Week 1-4

Describe what is going well in your internship experience…

Describe what you are doing well as an intern…

Describe what you would like to do better as an intern…

Describe what support or resources you need to improve your internship experience…

Track Your Progress

List your projects, tasks, and accomplishments in week 1 to 4:

Action Plan

Create 3 action steps to improve, adjust, or deepen your professional skills:

Celebrate

Celebrate every milestone, big and small. How will you celebrate all that you have accomplished so far?

Week 5: Building and Maintaining Professional Relationships
Your Network is Similar to a Garden...

You must tend to it consistently, and as flowers and plants produce clean air and other environmental benefits, so too will your networks. It is a reciprocal process that thrives on authentic relationships and support.

Strategies to Build Your Network

- Attend and volunteer at community, professional, and academic events
- LinkedIn connections - connect with people you have worked with and taken classes with
- Ask people in your network to introduce you to others
- Message people after you accept their connection or when they accept yours
- Leave recommendations and endorsements for others
- Smile and express openness to meeting and interacting
- During the meeting - say their name correctly at least one time
- Shake hands and make eye contact (if culturally acceptable)
- Say "Nice to meet you" when meeting someone new
- Say "Take care" when departing from your meeting
- Introduce yourself
- Exchange business cards

Strategies to Maintain Your Network

- Send a "thank you" note to follow-up
- Add them on LinkedIn
- Share updates about your accomplishments, next steps, new jobs, etc.
- Connect them with reputable individuals in your network
- Share resources, events and opportunities
- Stay engaged regarding their individual or organizational updates

Timeline

- Send a thank you card or message within 3-5 business days after meeting
- It's never too late to send a "thank you" message
- Share a memorable fact about yourself or your interaction to remind them of who you are (this is helpful after large events and for well-known leaders and professionals)

Weekly Check-In Meeting

Date/Time_____

Check-In

Talk with your supervisor about how you are doing, how your classes are going, and how your internship is going so far.

Report Your Progress

Bring updates regarding your progress on completed tasks and projects, as well as progress on ongoing work. Take notes and repeat any timelines, due dates, and clarify expectations for task or project completion.

Ask for Feedback

Ask for feedback from your supervisor about what you are doing well and which areas you could improve your performance. Ask your supervisor for any resources or additional information to support any areas of growth .

Ask for Support

Ask your supervisor for additional resources or support to support your internship experience.

Celebrate

Celebrate your accomplishments and growth, even if they seem incremental at times.

Summarize

Take notes of any tasks, due dates, upcoming meetings and events, and any other important items in need of follow-up.

Week 6: Networking

Definition of Networking

Networking includes making connections with new people, increasing your presence in the community and profession, and maintaining these relationships and your presence.

Philosophy Behind Networking

- Employers hire people that they can be sure of
- Building an awareness of your positive reputation
- Establish yourself as a professional
- Your networking efforts add value to your accomplishments on paper

Networking Strategies

- Do your "homework" prior to networking events or first meetings:
  - Lookup people on LinkedIn
  - Locate 1-3 "small talk" topics or experiences to discuss
- Be the first to say "hello"
- Take your breaks in areas where others naturally join together
- How to keep conversations going:
  - "Tell me more about that."
  - "I see that you are connected with Dr. Samira. We know each other from..."

Networking for Introverts

- Know your limits to social settings
- Practice your answers to these questions:
  - Who am I?
  - What brings me to this event or location?
  - What are my relevant interests and skills?
- Prepare yourself:
  - Practice deep breathing before entering the space (to calm your nerves)
  - Set goals (e.g. "I will introduce myself to 3 new people today.")
  - Bring networking or business cards and a pen
- Take notes on any business cards you receive from new connection (date, event, and any notes about who they are, their interests, etc.)

Weekly Check-In Meeting   Date/Time_____

Check-In
Talk with your supervisor about how you are doing, how your classes are going, and how your internship is going so far.

Report Your Progress
Bring updates regarding your progress on completed tasks and projects, as well as progress on ongoing work. Take notes and repeat any timelines, due dates, and clarify expectations for task or project completion.

Ask for Feedback
Ask for feedback from your supervisor about what you are doing well and which areas you could improve your performance. Ask your supervisor for any resources or additional information to support any areas of growth .

Ask for Support
Ask your supervisor for additional resources or support to support your internship experience.

Celebrate
Celebrate your accomplishments and growth, even if they seem incremental at times.

Summarize
Take notes of any tasks, due dates, upcoming meetings and events, and any other important items in need of follow-up.

Week 7: Stress Management

Definition

Monitoring and managing the amounts and types of stress in your life is essential to succeed personally, academically, and professionally. The goal is not to eliminate stress 100% because stress in lower amounts and in moderation can be healthy. Gauge your overall stress in combination with healthy coping strategies.

Stress Management Tips

Coping is a habit. Habits are similar to a muscle that you develop and strengthen through repetition. Practice coping strategies to build healthy habits in response to daily stressors in your life.

Here are several health coping strategies:
- Journaling
- Support network guidance
- Accountability buddies
- Positive self-talk
- Exercise
- Healthy food
- Hydration

Reflection

Which other coping strategies do you use to deal with stress?

Stress Management Activity

Make a stress ball using a balloon and flower or dry rice. Keep this stress ball to release stress in busy times.

Weekly Check-In Meeting

Date/Time_____

Check-In

Talk with your supervisor about how you are doing, how your classes are going, and how your internship is going so far.

Report Your Progress

Bring updates regarding your progress on completed tasks and projects, as well as progress on ongoing work. Take notes and repeat any timelines, due dates, and clarify expectations for task or project completion.

Ask for Feedback

Ask for feedback from your supervisor about what you are doing well and which areas you could improve your performance. Ask your supervisor for any resources or additional information to support any areas of growth .

Ask for Support

Ask your supervisor for additional resources or support to support your internship experience.

Celebrate

Celebrate your accomplishments and growth, even if they seem incremental at times.

Summarize

Take notes of any tasks, due dates, upcoming meetings and events, and any other important items in need of follow-up.

Week 8: Receiving and Processing Feedback

What is Constructive Feedback?

It is information provided by colleagues, supervisors, mentors, and other credible sources about your professionalism with the goal of enhancing and addressing behaviors in the professional environment, context, or sector.

Communicating in the Workplace

Internships are the prime place to learn new strategies, grow your skill sets, and start to incorporate feedback effectively

Don't Take it Personally

You are entering the professional world and it often comes with new ways of interacting, communicating, and expressing yourself. Here are some strategies you might find helpful.

- Approach it as a learning opportunity
- View feedback objectively
- Reflect on learnings
- Self-reflection is key
- Integrate feedback into your practice

Contact your internship supervisor for feedback and guidance. Consult with mentors, professors, elders, and community leaders for constructive feedback as well.

Acting on Feedback

- Gratitude
- Reflection
- Evaluation
- Integration
- Growth and expansion

Activity

Practice these feedback statements aloud:

- "Thank you for your feedback. I am always looking to grow as a professional."
- "I appreciate your feedback. Thank you for investing in my growth."
- "Thank you. I will integrate your feedback moving forward."
- "Thank you. I value your feedback."

Weekly Check-In Meeting   Date/Time_____

Check-In

Talk with your supervisor about how you are doing, how your classes are going, and how your internship is going so far.

Report Your Progress

Bring updates regarding your progress on completed tasks and projects, as well as progress on ongoing work. Take notes and repeat any timelines, due dates, and clarify expectations for task or project completion.

Ask for Feedback

Ask for feedback from your supervisor about what you are doing well and which areas you could improve your performance. Ask your supervisor for any resources or additional information to support any areas of growth .

Ask for Support

Ask your supervisor for additional resources or support to support your internship experience.

Celebrate

Celebrate your accomplishments and growth, even if they seem incremental at times.

Summarize

Take notes of any tasks, due dates, upcoming meetings and events, and any other important items in need of follow-up.

Quarter 2 Check-In: Week 5-8
Goals
Re-state and evaluate your goals from week 4 (page 20). Make any necessary adjustments and write them below:

Goals	Progress Notes
1. *Personal*	
2. *Academic*	
3. *Professional*	

Habits
Re-state and evaluate your habits from week 4 (page 20). Make any necessary adjustments and write them below:

Habits	Progress Notes
1. *Personal*	
2. *Academic*	
3. *Professional*	

Quarter 2 Self-Reflection: Week 5-8

Describe what is going well in your internship experience...

Describe what you are doing well as an intern...

Describe what you would like to do better as an intern...

Describe what support or resources you need to improve your internship experience...

Track Your Progress

List your projects, tasks, and accomplishments in week 5 to 8:

Action Plan

Create 3 action steps to improve, adjust, or deepen your professional skills:

Celebrate

Celebrate every milestone, big and small. How will you celebrate all that you have accomplished so far?

Week 9: Documenting Your Professional Accomplishments

Tracking Your Progress

- Projects
- Tasks
- Responsibilities
- Roles

Remember to include specific percentages, numbers, growth, output, impact, and project completion details.

Use High Impact Verbs

Here are several words to make your resume stand out:

- Influenced
- Created
- Launched
- Improved
- Achieved
- Resolved
- Managed

Activity

Create a LinkedIn profile (or enhance your existing profile).
Use these strategies:

- Add basic contact information
- Customize your profile's URL
- Add work experience and education information
- List as many relevant skills as possible
- Upload a professional headshot and tagline to describe yourself

Share your profile with your supervisor and ask for feedback. Integrate their feedback, then invite them to connect on LinkedIn.

Taking Your LinkedIn Profile to the Next Level

- Join groups in your professional field of interest
- Endorse others
- Provide recommendations for others
- Share important news in your professional field of interest
- Write your own professional content and share

Weekly Check-In Meeting   Date/Time_____

Check-In

Talk with your supervisor about how you are doing, how your classes are going, and how your internship is going so far.

Report Your Progress

Bring updates regarding your progress on completed tasks and projects, as well as progress on ongoing work. Take notes and repeat any timelines, due dates, and clarify expectations for task or project completion.

Ask for Feedback

Ask for feedback from your supervisor about what you are doing well and which areas you could improve your performance. Ask your supervisor for any resources or additional information to support any areas of growth .

Ask for Support

Ask your supervisor for additional resources or support to support your internship experience.

Celebrate

Celebrate your accomplishments and growth, even if they seem incremental at times.

Summarize

Take notes of any tasks, due dates, upcoming meetings and events, and any other important items in need of follow-up.

Week 10: Developing Your Vision Statement

What is a Vision Statement?

Your vision statement is a deeper dive into your goals. It is grounded in your values, passion, and purpose. Your vision statement details the ideal life you see and desire for yourself.

Reflection Activity

Reflect on each of the following before developing your vision statement:

What are the **values**, or the principles and guiding commitments you live by each day?

What are you **passionate** about?

What is your **purpose**? What were you born to accomplish?

Free-Write Activity

1. Get a blank sheet of paper. Engage in a 5-minute free-write activity to write all the details of the ideal life you see and desire. Write as many things that you can think of. Do not filter out any ideas in the free-write stage.
2. Now, write a 1-paragraph summary of your vision. Keep these items in mind:
   - Personal: Use "I", "Me", and "Myself" in your statement
   - Present Tense: Write it as if it's already happening today,
   - Positive Tone: use positive language, rather than "don't" or "not"
   - Passionate: Include emotions and feelings
   - Purpose: You must state your "Why?" or the reasons driving your vision

Create a Visual Cue

Post your vision statement somewhere where you will see it as you move about your daily life. You have just created a visual cue, or a physical reminder of your commitment to success.

Weekly Check-In Meeting

Date/Time_____

Check-In

Talk with your supervisor about how you are doing, how your classes are going, and how your internship is going so far.

Report Your Progress

Bring updates regarding your progress on completed tasks and projects, as well as progress on ongoing work. Take notes and repeat any timelines, due dates, and clarify expectations for task or project completion.

Ask for Feedback

Ask for feedback from your supervisor about what you are doing well and which areas you could improve your performance. Ask your supervisor for any resources or additional information to support any areas of growth .

Ask for Support

Ask your supervisor for additional resources or support to support your internship experience.

Celebrate

Celebrate your accomplishments and growth, even if they seem incremental at times.

Summarize

Take notes of any tasks, due dates, upcoming meetings and events, and any other important items in need of follow-up.

Week 11: Your Personal Brand Statement

Definition

Your personal brand is your reputation and the value that you provide. It corresponds with how you want to be known and what you would like to be known for. Your brand statement is simply a concise description of your current and aspirational reputation.

Purpose

Your personal brand statement is useful in providing talking points about yourself for current and future opportunities. It is a result of your daily decisions and behaviors in personal, academic, and professional settings. Sometimes called a "promise of value" statement, it describes your unique skills and contributions.

Self-Reflection

What value do you provide? What type of change and impact do you influence? (your value)

What is unique about the way that you promote change and influence impact? (your distinction)

Who do you impact? (your audience)

Activity

In 1-2 sentences, create a concise personal brand statement and write it below:

Your personal brand statement will comprise the beginning of your elevator speech in next week's lesson.

Weekly Check-In Meeting   Date/Time_____

Check-In

Talk with your supervisor about how you are doing, how your classes are going, and how your internship is going so far.

Report Your Progress

Bring updates regarding your progress on completed tasks and projects, as well as progress on ongoing work. Take notes and repeat any timelines, due dates, and clarify expectations for task or project completion.

Ask for Feedback

Ask for feedback from your supervisor about what you are doing well and which areas you could improve your performance. Ask your supervisor for any resources or additional information to support any areas of growth .

Ask for Support

Ask your supervisor for additional resources or support to support your internship experience.

Celebrate

Celebrate your accomplishments and growth, even if they seem incremental at times.

Summarize

Take notes of any tasks, due dates, upcoming meetings and events, and any other important items in need of follow-up.

Week 12: Crafting Your Elevator Speech
What is an Elevator Speech?

An elevator speech is a 30-second pitch about yourself to use during networking events, interviews, and in professional settings. It lets potential employers and other professionals know how your experience and skills can benefit their organization, and informs others how to support your goals.

An elevator speech includes:
- Relevant experience and accomplishments
- Your skills and strengths
- Your goals

Reflection Questions:

What are your accomplishments and areas of experience?

What are your skills and strengths?

Which goals are you working towards?

What keeps you motivated toward your goals?

Elevator Speech Activity

Write 3-4 sentences that include at least one answer from each of the questions above. Remember to add your personal brand statement from last week to the beginning of your elevator speech.

Weekly Check-In Meeting

Date/Time_____

Check-In

Talk with your supervisor about how you are doing, how your classes are going, and how your internship is going so far.

Report Your Progress

Bring updates regarding your progress on completed tasks and projects, as well as progress on ongoing work. Take notes and repeat any timelines, due dates, and clarify expectations for task or project completion.

Ask for Feedback

Ask for feedback from your supervisor about what you are doing well and which areas you could improve your performance. Ask your supervisor for any resources or additional information to support any areas of growth .

Ask for Support

Ask your supervisor for additional resources or support to support your internship experience.

Celebrate

Celebrate your accomplishments and growth, even if they seem incremental at times.

Summarize

Take notes of any tasks, due dates, upcoming meetings and events, and any other important items in need of follow-up.

Quarter 3 Check-In: Week 9-12

Evaluating Your Goals:

Re-state and evaluate your goals from week 8 (page 30). Make any necessary adjustments and write them below:

Goals	Progress Notes
1. *Personal*	
2. *Academic*	
3. *Professional*	

Evaluating Your Habits:

Re-state and evaluate your habits from week 8 (page 30). Make any necessary adjustments and write them below:

Habits	Progress Notes
1. *Personal*	
2. *Academic*	
3. *Professional*	

Quarter 3 Self-Reflection: Week 9-12

Describe what is going well in your internship experience…

Describe what you are doing well as an intern…

Describe what you would like to do better as an intern…

Describe what support or resources you need to improve your internship experience…

Track Your Progress
List your projects, tasks, and accomplishments in week 9 to 12:

Action Plan
Create 3 action steps to improve, adjust, or deepen your professional skills:

Celebrate
Celebrate every milestone, big and small. How will you celebrate all that you have accomplished so far?

Week 13: Writing Your Career Goal Statement

What is a Career Goal Statement?

A career goal statement includes:

- Short and long-term career goals
- Previous career accomplishments
- Current qualifications and experience

Reflection Activity

What are my short-term and long-term career aspirations?

Why am I drawn to this career path?

How do my values align with this career path?

What do I hope to accomplish?

What are my previous accomplishments?

What are my current qualifications and experience related to this career path?

Writing Your Career Goal Statement

Create 2-3 sentences that detail your career goals and write it below:

Weekly Check-In Meeting   Date/Time_____

Check-In

Talk with your supervisor about how you are doing, how your classes are going, and how your internship is going so far.

Report Your Progress

Bring updates regarding your progress on completed tasks and projects, as well as progress on ongoing work. Take notes and repeat any timelines, due dates, and clarify expectations for task or project completion.

Ask for Feedback

Ask for feedback from your supervisor about what you are doing well and which areas you could improve your performance. Ask your supervisor for any resources or additional information to support any areas of growth .

Ask for Support

Ask your supervisor for additional resources or support to support your internship experience.

Celebrate

Celebrate your accomplishments and growth, even if they seem incremental at times.

Summarize

Take notes of any tasks, due dates, upcoming meetings and events, and any other important items in need of follow-up.

Week 14: Communicating Your Experience and Next Steps
Crafting Your Narrative

- Who you are
- Experiences before the internship
- Transformation and accomplishments
- Habit formation
- Aspirations
- Next steps

Reflection Activity

Who are you today?

Who do you aspire to be?

Describe your accomplishments and your overall transformation as a student intern?

Which areas of professional growth would you like to seek growth in?

Which areas of professional growth would you like to continue to grow in?

What are your next steps in the near future? Long-term?

Write Your Narrative

Create 2-3 sentences describing your responses above in a concise format and write it below:

Weekly Check-In Meeting   Date/Time_____

Check-In

Talk with your supervisor about how you are doing, how your classes are going, and how your internship is going so far.

Report Your Progress

Bring updates regarding your progress on completed tasks and projects, as well as progress on ongoing work. Take notes and repeat any timelines, due dates, and clarify expectations for task or project completion.

Ask for Feedback

Ask for feedback from your supervisor about what you are doing well and which areas you could improve your performance. Ask your supervisor for any resources or additional information to support any areas of growth .

Ask for Support

Ask your supervisor for additional resources or support to support your internship experience.

Celebrate

Celebrate your accomplishments and growth, even if they seem incremental at times.

Summarize

Take notes of any tasks, due dates, upcoming meetings and events, and any other important items in need of follow-up.

Week 15: Transitioning From Your Internship
Goals

When transitioning from your internship, your goals should be to:
- Leave a positive and lasting impression with your supervisor, colleagues, and peers
- Reflect on what you have learned and accomplished
- Communicate these learnings and accomplishments
- Express gratitude to those who have supported or impacted you
- Make a plan for the future (staying in touch at a future event, setting up follow-up meetings, connecting on LinkedIn, etc.)
- Communicate your plan for the future (sharing your aspirations, your next steps, and sharing resources)
- Finish strong by completing any assignments and communicating any necessary updates

Closure

As you depart from your internship role, here are some strategies to keep in mind to assist your supervisor in this process:
- Close out any existing projects and turn over documents and updates to team members
- Communicate next steps for long-term projects
- Turn in any keys, passwords, equipment, parking, and ID cards
- Provide contact information to others so you may stay connected
- Share your learnings and feedback with your supervisor

Gratitude

Practice gratitude in these ways, among others:
- Prepare thank you cards or letters
- Schedule in-person meetings to share your gratitude
- Provide LinkedIn recommendations for professionals who have impacted you

Weekly Check-In Meeting   Date/Time_____

Check-In

Talk with your supervisor about how you are doing, how your classes are going, and how your internship is going so far.

Report Your Progress

Bring updates regarding your progress on completed tasks and projects, as well as progress on ongoing work. Take notes and repeat any timelines, due dates, and clarify expectations for task or project completion.

Ask for Feedback

Ask for feedback from your supervisor about what you are doing well and which areas you could improve your performance. Ask your supervisor for any resources or additional information to support any areas of growth .

Ask for Support

Ask your supervisor for additional resources or support to support your internship experience.

Celebrate

Celebrate your accomplishments and growth, even if they seem incremental at times.

Summarize

Take notes of any tasks, due dates, upcoming meetings and events, and any other important items in need of follow-up.

Week 16: Letters of Recommendation and Cover Letters

Letters of Recommendation

People who are respected in the field can vouch for your professionalism with letters of recommendation. They communicate that other organizations should hire you. Letters of recommendation outline your skills, professionalism, and accomplishments.

How to Ask for a Letter of Recommendation

- Asking the question: "Would you be willing to write a positive letter of recommendation for me?"
- Give 4-6 weeks advance notice
- Clarify whether this is a general letter of recommendation or if its for a specific scholarship, job, or other opportunity
- Provide an details regarding the submission of the letter

Self-Reflection

If you were asked to write a letter of recommendation for yourself, what would you write?

Activity

Brainstorm 1-3 people who can provide a positive professional letter of recommendation for you and note what they would say about you:

Name	What would they say about you?

Week 16: Letters of Recommendation and Cover Letters

Resume vs. Cover Letter

- **Resume:** A detailed list of your work and education experience, skills and accomplishments
- **Cover Letter:** A summary of your highlighted qualifications for the specific position and organization written in the format of a letter

Important Cover Letter Reminders

- Research the position and the organization
- Customize each cover letter with this specific information
- Summarize your experience in 3 bullets, then expand on each
  (Tip: These should match the qualifications listed in the job description)
- Provide stories and examples that demonstrate your experience and skills
- Explain how you will benefit the employer and the organization's goals

Transferrable Skills

Connect past experience and skills to this opportunity.

> *For example: customer services experience, class assignments, volunteer experience and skills that can be applied to this career*

Self-Promotion

You must believe your are the best candidate for the position. Your cover letter should communicate this. It is perfectly okay to brag about your accomplishments with specific, professional language and examples

Logistics

- Clean format, simple font, and easy-to-read
- Proof read to ensure no typos or misspellings
- Keep it less than one page in length at early stages of your career
- Follow application instructions and deadlines very closely
- Save an editable document for your records
- Submit a PDF version of documents (maintains formatting)

Weekly Check-In Meeting   Date/Time_____

Check-In

Talk with your supervisor about how you are doing, how your classes are going, and how your internship is going so far.

Report Your Progress

Bring updates regarding your progress on completed tasks and projects, as well as progress on ongoing work. Take notes and repeat any timelines, due dates, and clarify expectations for task or project completion.

Ask for Feedback

Ask for feedback from your supervisor about what you are doing well and which areas you could improve your performance. Ask your supervisor for any resources or additional information to support any areas of growth .

Ask for Support

Ask your supervisor for additional resources or support to support your internship experience.

Celebrate

Celebrate your accomplishments and growth, even if they seem incremental at times.

Summarize

Take notes of any tasks, due dates, upcoming meetings and events, and any other important items in need of follow-up.

Notes

Quarter 4 Check-In: Week 13-16

Goals

Re-state and evaluate your goals from week 12 (page 40). Making any necessary adjustments and write them below:

Goals	Progress Notes
1. *Personal*	
2. *Academic*	
3. *Professional*	

Habits

Re-state and evaluate your habits from week 12 (page 40). Make any necessary adjustments and write them below:

Habits	Progress Notes
1. *Personal*	
2. *Academic*	
3. *Professional*	

Quarter 4 Self-Reflection: Week 13-16

Describe what is going well in your internship experience...

Describe what you are doing well as an intern...

Describe what you would like to do better as an intern...

Describe the support or resources you need to improve your internship experience...

Track Your Progress
List your projects, tasks, and accomplishments in week 13-16:

Action Plan
Create action steps to improve, adjust, or deepen your professional skills:

Celebrate
Celebrate every milestone, big and small. How will you celebrate all that you have accomplished so far?

Post-Internship
Overall Self-Reflection

You have now worked for 16 weeks in this role as an intern. Reflecting on your overall journey is a key ingredient to intentional growth and development.

What have you learned?

What have you contributed?

What types of tasks and roles do you love completing or performing?

Do you see yourself in a future professional role similar to this one?
Why or why not?

Post-Internship
Overall Self-Reflection

Which careers are you now interested in?

What have you done extremely well over the last 16 weeks?

If given another opportunity, what would you have done differently?

If given another opportunity, what would you have done exactly the same (because it led to success)?

Post-Internship

Reflecting on Your Career Readiness Competencies

Reflect on the skills, experience, and knowledge you have gained in each of these career readiness competency areas. Given that employers are looking for recent college graduates with these skills, be sure to highlight these accomplishments and skills in your resume and cover letters where it is relevant to do so. Be sure to list any specific projects, initiatives, and outcomes.

Critical thinking and Problem Solving: *Exercise sound reasoning to analyze issues, make decisions, and overcome problems*

Professionalism: *Demonstrate personal accountability and effective work habits*

Teamwork and Collaboration: *Build collaborative relationships with colleagues and customers representing diverse cultures, races, ages, genders, religions, lifestyles, and viewpoints*

Oral and Written Communication: *Articulate thoughts and ideas clearly and effectively in written and oral forms to persons inside and outside of the organization*

(Source: National Association of Colleges and Employers)

Post-Internship

Continuing Your Growth and Experience
Self-Reflection

How will you continue growing and developing for a future career?

Additional Strategies

1. Taking it Back to Campus

Here are several campus resources for you to consider partnering with at your college or university:

- Career Services
- Advising
- Counseling
- Leadership Development
- Student Life & Involvement
- Athletics
- Campus Employment

2. Mentor Others

There are many ways to pay forward your learning and experience to others. Here are a few ideas:

- Seek other paid and volunteer opportunities to contribute to the field
- Recommend other students participate in internship programs
- Share your experiences and opportunities with family members

3. Engage with Your Host Organization

Remain an active member of the professional community and contribute to the future growth of the organization.

- **Staff**: Connect on LinkedIn
- **Other colleagues and interns**: Share resources, events, jobs, grants, scholarships, and volunteer opportunities
- **Future interns**: Share guidance and lessons learned with future interns.

Post-Internship
Continuing Your Growth and Experience
Additional Resources for Student Interns
- "Her Campus Internship Guide 2016"
  http://www.hercampus.com/tag/internship-guide-2016
- "How To Balance Working And Going To College" article
  Author: Michelle Schroeder-Gardner
  http://www.makingsenseofcents.com/2015/10/tips-for-working-students-in-college.html
- Top Job Skills for Employees resource collection
  http://www.job-interview-site.com/Job-Interviewing-tips/management-leadership-skills

Growing Your Professional Skills
Check out these sources for webinars, online courses, and other professional development resources to grow your professional skills:

- Lynda
- Udemy
- Coursera
- SkillShare
- iTunesU
- Khan Academy
- Brioxy

Your campus is also a fantastic source of development opportunities. Your campus career center, student life, and other departments will offer workshops and opportunities to sharpen your leadership and professional skill sets.

Activity
Create a professional development plan. It can be helpful to guide future professional decisions and seek areas of future opportunity.

Locate a professional development plan template online that fits your needs. One possible resource is:

"Creating Your Professional Development Plan: The 10-Step Process"
EatYourCareer.com

Post-Internship
Deepening Your Career Readiness Competencies

Here are some additional resources for you to continue to develop and deepen your skill sets:

Resume Writing

"7 Habits That'll Take Your Resume to the Next Level" article
Megan Sweet, HerCampus.com, April 3, 2016

Cover Letter Writing

"A Strategy for Writing the Dreaded Cover Letter"
Katharine Brooks, Ed.D, PsychologyToday.com, April 8, 2011

Networking

"Networking for the Novice, Nervous, or Naïve Job Seekers" book
Tom Dezell

LinkedIn

"How to Use LinkedIn: 35 LinkedIn Tips for Professional Networking, Business and Marketing"
Pamela Vaughan, HubSpot.com

Habits

"Transform Your Habits" e-book
James Clear

Communication

"Taking Constructive Criticism Like a Champ" article
Nicole Lindsay, TheMuse.com

Career Search & Interviewing

The Muse blog and newsletter, TheMuse.com

Personal Brand

"Your Personal Brand Workbook" e-book
PricewaterhouseCoopers(PwC)

Informational Interviews

"Your Complete Guide to Informational Interviews"
Rachel Gates, HerCampus.com, April 3, 2013

STUDENT INTERNSHIP SUCCESS WORKBOOK   Copyright © 2017 Resilient Campus LLC

59